GAUTAMA BUDDHA

GAUTAMA BUDDHA

ODYSSEYS

MELISSA GISH

CREATIVE EDUCATION · CREATIVE PAPERBACKS

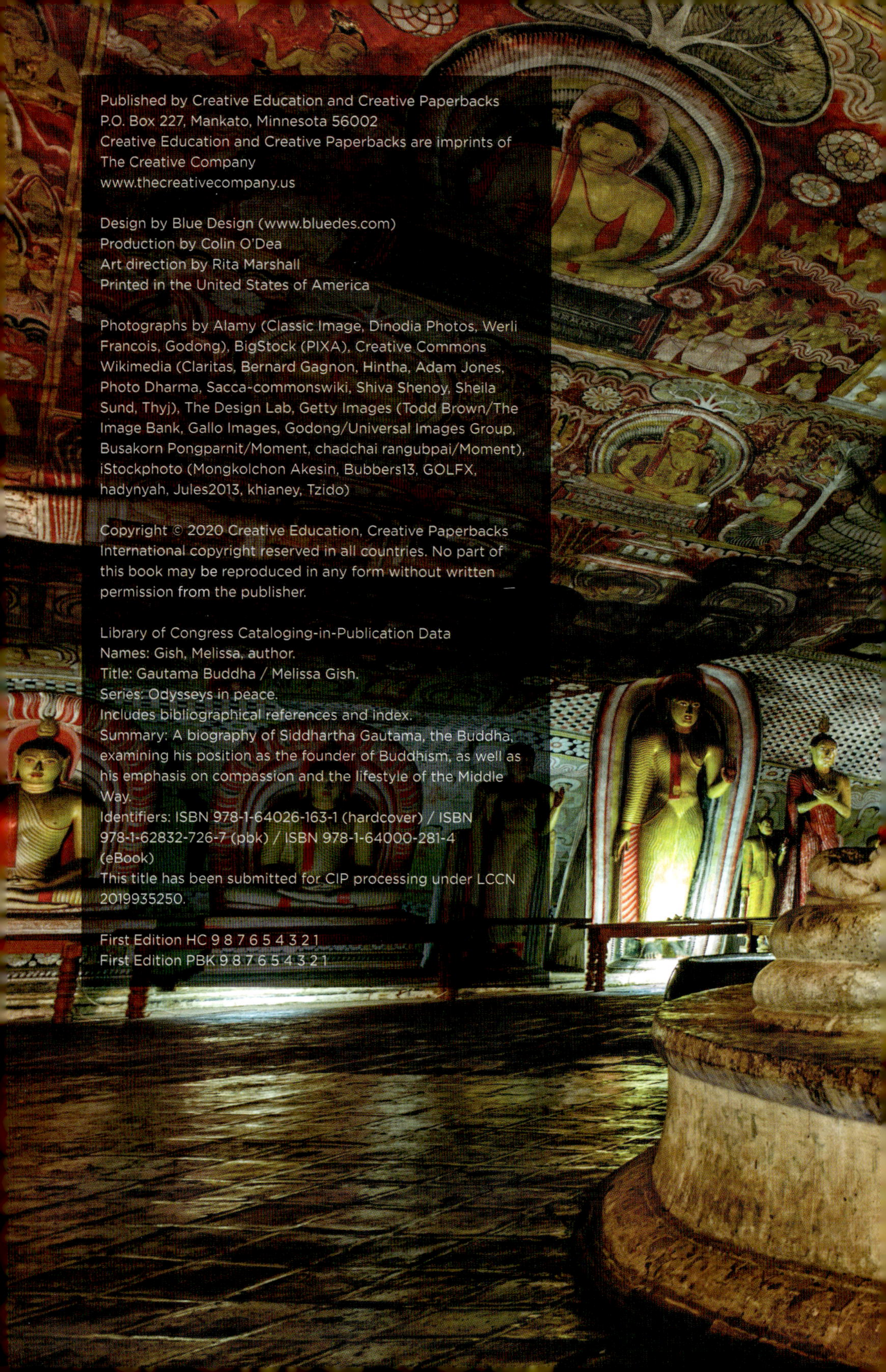

Published by Creative Education and Creative Paperbacks
P.O. Box 227, Mankato, Minnesota 56002
Creative Education and Creative Paperbacks are imprints of The Creative Company
www.thecreativecompany.us

Design by Blue Design (www.bluedes.com)
Production by Colin O'Dea
Art direction by Rita Marshall
Printed in the United States of America

Photographs by Alamy (Classic Image, Dinodia Photos, Werli Francois, Godong), BigStock (PIXA), Creative Commons Wikimedia (Claritas, Bernard Gagnon, Hintha, Adam Jones, Photo Dharma, Sacca-commonswiki, Shiva Shenoy, Sheila Sund, Thyj), The Design Lab, Getty Images (Todd Brown/The Image Bank, Gallo Images, Godong/Universal Images Group, Busakorn Pongparnit/Moment, chadchai rangubpai/Moment), iStockphoto (Mongkolchon Akesin, Bubbers13, GOLFX, hadynyah, Jules2013, khianey, Tzido)

Library of Congress Cataloging-in-Publication Data
Names: Gish, Melissa, author.
Title: Gautama Buddha / Melissa Gish.
Series: Odysseys in peace.
Includes bibliographical references and index.
Summary: A biography of Siddhartha Gautama, the Buddha, examining his position as the founder of Buddhism, as well as his emphasis on compassion and the lifestyle of the Middle Way.
Identifiers: ISBN 978-1-64026-163-1 (hardcover) / ISBN 978-1-62832-726-7 (pbk) / ISBN 978-1-64000-281-4 (eBook)
This title has been submitted for CIP processing under LCCN 2019935250.

First Edition HC 9 8 7 6 5 4 3 2 1
First Edition PBK 9 8 7 6 5 4 3 2 1

CONTENTS

Introduction

More than 2,500 years ago, in what is now southern Nepal, a person was born who became known as the Buddha, a title that means "the awakened one." Today, he is revered around the world as one of the most important religious figures in the history of humankind. Buddhism is the world's fourth-largest religion, with more than half a billion followers from nearly every nation around the globe. Although no one today seriously

OPPOSITE: Statues of Buddha around the globe not only serve as reminders of Buddha's peaceful and compassionate teachings but also may be tributes to other influential people who had them built.

OPPOSITE At Angkor Wat in Cambodia, a community of Buddhists lives in a sprawling temple complex that was originally built for Hindus but has been Buddhist since the late 1100s.

questions Buddha's historical existence, little about his life is known for certain. Many stories of Buddha's experiences have been remembered and retold, repeated countless times, collected and interpreted by scholars and religious experts, and written and rewritten until they were eventually accepted as the history of Buddha.

Because Buddha emphasized the importance of cultural relativism in his teachings, there is much variation in the interpretation of his principles and the structure and practice of the religious community he founded. There is also disagreement about the very nature and identity of Buddha himself. But all accounts of Buddha portray him as a wise, compassionate person who led by example. Inspired by Buddha and his guiding principle of compassion, Buddhists today continue to not only seek their own escape from suffering but also actively help others find peace in their lives.

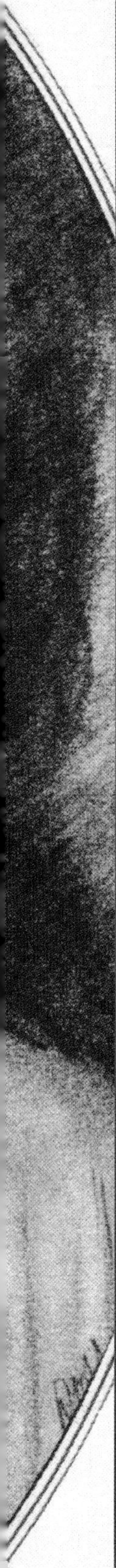

Life as a Prince

Siddhartha (*sid-AR-tuh*) Gautama (*guh-TAH-muh*) is believed to have been born about 563 B.C. in the ancient city of Lumbini. His family practiced **Hinduism**. The circumstances of his birth are known only from stories that were passed along orally at first and later written. Many stories of Siddhartha's beginnings are fictionalized **myths** based on actual events. According to one common story, Siddhartha's mother, Maya, had

OPPOSITE: In addition to the names Siddhartha Gautama and Gautama Buddha, the Buddha is also known as Shakyamuni Buddha, or the historical Buddha, after the Shakya kingdom into which he was born.

OPPOSITE The legendary birth story of Buddha includes the tradition that the newborn walked seven steps and proclaimed that he would become enlightened, ending suffering for others.

a dream in which Siddhartha is conceived. In the dream, a beautiful white elephant with six tusks—the symbol of greatness—gives Maya a white lotus blossom. The elephant then enters the right side of Maya's body, and a baby begins to grow. Ten months later, as was customary at the time, Maya left home to give birth at her father's palace. On the way, she stopped to bathe and rest. Then, as she stood under a sal tree, the tree lowered a branch toward Maya. She reached up and grasped the branch. Steadying herself, she gave birth. But the birth was unusual: a baby boy emerged from Maya's side.

Maya returned with her newborn to her husband, Suddhodana, in Kapilavastu, an ancient city somewhere around the border of India and Nepal that no longer exists today. Some stories say that Suddhodana was a king. Others say he was an elected tribal chief. Regardless, he

India's Caste System

For more than 2,500 years, Hindus in India lived in a **caste** system, which divided people into four social groups that did not mix. Though illegal today, this tradition is still practiced by many Hindus, who refuse to work or marry outside the caste into which they were born. Brahmans, the scholars and priests, were the most important people. Below them were Kshatriyas (*kuh-SHAT-tree-yas*), the warriors and kings. This was the caste of Siddhartha's family. Next were the Vaisyas (*VY-shee-yas*), the farmers and merchants. The bottom caste was the Sudras (*SOO-drus*), the servants and laborers. A fifth group of people, the Dalits, also called the untouchables, were the social outcasts.

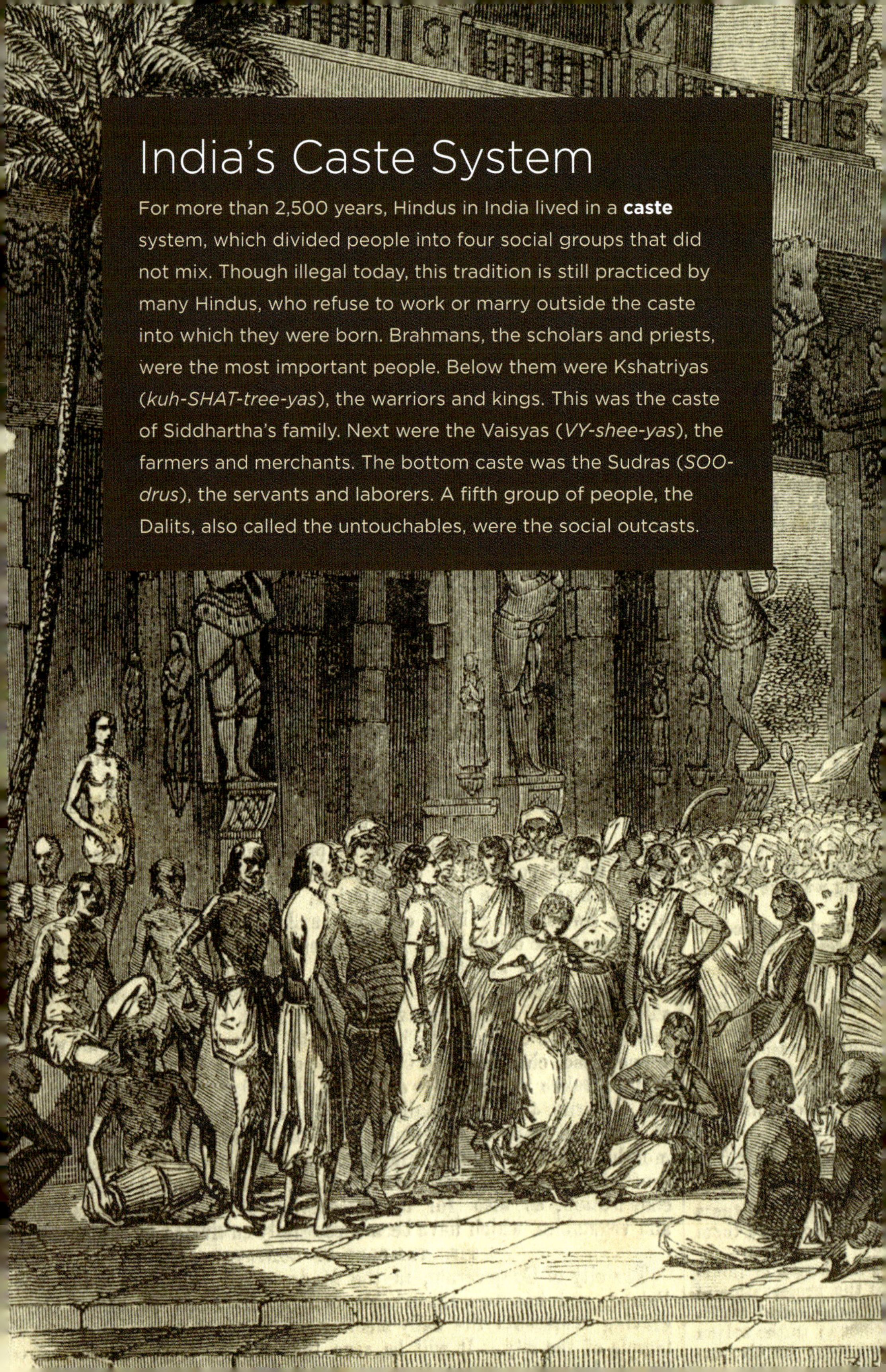

owned several palaces, and his clan, the Shakyas, held a vast territory. On the fifth day after their son's birth, the happy couple held a naming ceremony at one of their palaces. They called their son Siddhartha, a name that means "he who achieves his goal." A sage named Asita came down from his mountain home to see the infant prince. He predicted that the boy would grow up to become either a king or a spiritual teacher. Suddhodana did not like this dual prediction, for he wished only for his son to inherit his kingdom. He invited eight wise men to the celebration, hoping for a different conclusion. Seven of the wise men made the same dual prediction. The eighth insisted that the boy would absolutely become a spiritual teacher.

Within days of the naming ceremony, tragedy struck the kingdom: Maya died. As was tradition, Suddhodana married Maya's sister, Mahaprajapati. Wishing to shield Siddhartha from any further sorrow—and protect him from the influence of religion—Suddhodana and Mahaprajapati raised the boy in complete isolation within the walls of their palaces—one for summer, one for winter, and one for the rainy season. They provided Siddhartha with every luxury, from servants and playmates to the finest clothing and food. They kept him healthy and happy, and they kept anyone who wasn't healthy or happy away from him. They also gave him siblings: a half-brother, Nanda, and a half-sister, Sundari Nanda.

Suddhodana's one wish for his eldest son was that

OPPOSITE Royals and other people of status in Siddhartha's time wore heavy earrings that stretched the earlobes; depictions of him before and after enlightenment almost always show this feature.

Siddhartha would one day rule all of India's 16 kingdoms as emperor. To make sure his son would never want to leave the palace, Suddhodana created for Siddhartha a life of pure pleasure. The boy feasted daily, and life was filled with constant entertainment, including music, dance, and traveling acrobats and theater troupes. His father kept religious teachings from him, and all forms of human suffering were hidden. Siddhartha knew nothing but joy.

When Siddhartha was 16, his father arranged his marriage to Yasodhara, Siddhartha's 15-year-old cousin. The two fell in love and were happy together for many years. When Siddhartha was 29, Yasodhara gave birth to a son, who was named Rahula. In his new role as a parent, Siddhartha felt compelled to meet the people that his family ruled. Despite his father's objections, he

BELOW Siddhartha's fact-finding missions from the palace showed him old age, illness, and death—all three represented at once in this painting from a Cambodian Buddhist monastery.

left the palace to travel the countryside. Along the way, he had a series of four encounters that would change his life. These are known as the "four sights."

Siddhartha left the palace in a chariot driven by his friend Channa and pulled by his favorite horse, a tall, white steed named Kanthaka. On his first journey beyond the palace walls, he met a toothless, frail old man. Not understanding what he was seeing, Siddhartha asked Channa to explain. Channa described how people change and grow old. It is the nature of the human body, Channa told Siddhartha, that we all weaken and become tired. All the way back to the palace that day, Siddhartha pondered the concept of aging. Later, Siddhartha asked Channa to take him to the countryside again. This time, they encountered a person stricken by disease, lying in his own excrement. Confounded, Siddhartha again asked Channa to explain. Channa told him that no one is immune from disease. Everyone gets sick, and everyone feels pain. Siddhartha was struck by this news and pondered it deeply. Wishing to see more, Siddhartha set out a third time. What he saw next was a bloated, dead body. He was shocked. Channa explained that no one escapes this fate. Life is fleeting; everyone dies.

These three sights weighed heavily on Siddhartha. He felt guilty that for so long he had lived a life of pleasure with no knowledge of the pain and suffering of others. He needed more answers. On his fourth trip, Siddhartha encountered an **ascetic**. This man was living a life that was in complete opposition to Siddhartha's. He lived in the forest. His clothes were modest, and he ate very little food. Yet the man was not unhappy. And even though he knew that he would eventually suffer and die, the man

CHINA
TIBET
NEPAL
LUMBINI
INDIA
BAY OF BENGAL
RABIAN SEA
INDIAN OCEAN

OPPOSITE After Siddhartha left her in the middle of the night to seek enlightenment, Yasodhara followed the news of her husband's new life and also gave up many comforts to imitate his example.

was happy with just being alive at that moment.

Back at his palace, Siddhartha grappled with what he had seen. How can people be happy when so much suffering exists? This puzzle weighed on his mind. He felt compelled to understand. One night, as he watched his wife and infant son sleep, his heart grew unbearably heavy. He knew that he could achieve peace only if he, too, sought understanding of human suffering. To do so, he would have to leave his family and his comfortable life in the palace. Stories tell of how Mara, the demon god of desire, tried to convince Siddhartha to stay by showing him visions of the great Indian empire that he could one day rule. But Siddhartha rejected Mara's temptation. Accompanied by Channa and Kanthaka, Siddhartha left the palace.

QUOTE

"Just as a storm cannot prevail against a rocky mountain, so Mara can never overpower the man who lives meditating on the impurities, who is controlled in his senses, moderate in eating, and filled with faith and earnest effort."

- Gautama Buddha, *Khuddaka Nikāya*

Path to Enlightenment

Far from his palace, Siddhartha took off his fancy clothes. He draped himself in a simple cotton robe and cut his hair. He ordered Channa to return to the palace with Kanthaka. Disavowing his wealth and heritage, Siddhartha adopted the life of a **mendicant**. Completely alone, he began walking south, stopping at night to sleep in orchards and forests with no shelter. He survived on food

OPPOSITE: A practice of some ascetics was to cut their hair when renouncing their former lives, which Siddhartha is shown doing in this painting about the start of his life as a mendicant.

that he received from strangers. Siddhartha encountered some Hindu priests performing rituals. They chanted in worship to the gods and **celestial** bodies. Many people in India suffered from widespread poverty and lived under the constant threat of violence and war. The priests explained to Siddhartha that their rituals would provide inner peace to the suffering masses. But many people felt their religion did not give them the spiritual peace they craved. Their priests' rituals felt like empty promises.

Siddhartha was not alone in giving up his past life in an effort to find spiritual fulfillment. Known as renunciants, thousands of people like Siddhartha renounced their material possessions and comforts in order to seek **enlightenment**. The renunciants' goal was to escape **Samsāra**. Prior to Siddhartha's birth from Maya, he believed he had lived many lives—some in animals and

Samsāra

Hinduism teaches that every living being passes through a series of lives that depend on karma (the balance of good and bad actions). This cycle is called Samsāra, a Sanskrit word meaning "wandering." Upon death, a person's karma is examined, and the form of his or her next being is decided. A person with bad karma is required to pay for bad deeds. This person may be reborn as an animal. After a number of lives as various animals, this person may be reborn as a human again. To break the cycle, this person must collect only good karma and achieve Nirvana, which is a state of perfect peace.

OPPOSITE As Siddhartha did long ago, modern mendicants gather near India's holy places such as Tamil Nadu's Mt. Arunachala, seeking alms.

some in people. Like other renunciants, Siddhartha sought a teacher to guide him on his spiritual quest for release from the endless cycle of death and rebirth. Siddhartha heard of a teacher named Ālāra Kālāma and was eager to meet him, so Siddhartha traveled to the city of Rajgir in the kingdom of Magadha. While begging, Siddhartha was spotted by King Bibbisara, who recognized that Siddhartha was no ordinary beggar. Upon questioning Siddhartha, the king realized that Siddhartha was the son of Suddhodana. In an act of political diplomacy, the king asked Siddhartha to join his kingdom. Siddhartha declined, explaining that he was on a spiritual journey to attain enlightenment. If Siddhartha succeeded in his quest, the king asked that he return to Magadha as a teacher one day. Siddhartha agreed and continued on his way.

Siddhartha found the guru (spiritual teacher) Ālāra Kālāma and became his pupil. Kālāma was a master of meditation. He taught Siddhartha techniques for focusing on a single thought to achieve a level of mental clarity that allowed him to be perfectly calm. Siddhartha learned quickly and soon matched his teacher's skills at meditation. Ultimately, Siddhartha was unsatisfied with his experience because the peace brought on by meditation was fleeting. He went in search of another teacher. Next, he found the guru Uddaka Rāmaputta. Once again, he easily exceeded his teacher's skills in meditation. Rāmaputta elevated Siddhartha to the status of teacher and stepped down into the role of pupil, worshiping Siddhartha and asking to be instructed by him. But Siddhartha felt that Rāmaputta's teachings

Ascetics believed that in experiencing an existence of suffering and near-death, they would be reborn as beings with a deep understanding of the human condition.

were not valuable enough, since they did not help him achieve a permanent state of inner peace and enlightenment. So Siddhartha abandoned Rāmaputta and sought a completely different approach.

Asceticism was commonly practiced by renunciants to attain wisdom. Ascetics believed that in experiencing an existence of suffering and near-death, they would be reborn as beings with a deep understanding of the human condition. Siddhartha joined five other ascetics in embracing the practice to the extreme. He ate barely a

The Three Poisons

Buddha taught that three destructive character flaws exist in all humans. He called them the Three Poisons: selfishness, anger, and ignorance. He knew that people who harbored these characteristics could never find peace in their lives. His teachings tell people to recognize their weaknesses and strive to overcome them with alternatives. He said, "Do not deny them; rather, embrace their opposition: instead of selfishness, cultivate generosity; instead of anger, cultivate compassion; instead of ignorance, cultivate wisdom."

spoonful of rice each day and drank only enough water to stay alive. He wore little clothing and did not even attempt to shelter himself from harsh cold or penetrating heat. He practiced **yoga** every waking moment, sometimes standing all day on one foot or lying on beds of nails. His goal in punishing his body in these ways was to lift his mind into a state of ultimate understanding of human suffering. His body wasted away. His skin turned dark under the beating sun. His hair thinned. In one translation of Siddhartha's own description of the experience, he said, "My spine stood forth like corded beads; my ribs jutted out as gaunt as the rafters of an old roofless barn; ... my scalp shriveled and withered as a green gourd shrivels and withers in the wind and sun." Indeed, after six years of self-torture, Siddhartha was perilously close to death.

However, he did not achieve the wisdom that he

sought. One day, as he was lying under a tree, Siddhartha drifted into a dream, recalling a time when he was a young boy. His father took him to the fields to celebrate the spring planting. People danced as the fields were dug up. Siddhartha looked down at his feet and watched the insects scatter. He realized that they were being destroyed by the planting, which made him sad. Stirring from the dream, Siddhartha felt engulfed in this harsh reality and suddenly understood that every living thing shares the life-and-death struggle of all other living things. The sadness he recalled from his dream turned into an overwhelming sense of pure joy. Realizing that this feeling of joy would be lost if he died, he recognized that asceticism was not the way to achieve enlightenment.

Various stories exist that describe what happened next. One story tells of a woman named Sujata who came

OPPOSITE In many images of Buddha meditating, he is shown with his hands resting atop his lap—left hand on right with fingers stretched out—in a mudra (symbolic gesture) called the dhyana mudra.

to the tree under which Siddhartha had dreamed. She brought a bowl of rice boiled in milk with the intention of presenting it as an offering to a tree-deity, whom she wished to thank for giving her a happy family. But when she saw Siddhartha so near death, she offered him the bowl instead. The food reminded Siddhartha of the rice pudding his stepmother had fed him as a child. Sujata's kind gesture reinforced Siddhartha's belief in the interconnectedness of everything and everyone. Looking to gurus and joining ascetics, Siddhartha had failed to find enlightenment. Now, he knew that the only place left to look was within himself. Accepting Sujata's gift of food, Siddhartha made the decision to restore his health and continue his quest.

QUOTE

"One truly is the protector of oneself; who else could the protector be? With oneself fully controlled, one gains a mastery that is hard to gain."

- Gautama Buddha, *Dhammapada*

The Awakened One

Some stories about Siddhartha's achievement of enlightenment tell how this event occurred suddenly one night under a full moon. Other stories explain a longer process that took 49 days. But all stories share one common element: the Bodhi tree. In the ancient town of Bodh Gaya, Siddhartha, now 35 years old and healthy again, sat under a fig tree to meditate. He had realized the interconnectedness of every living

OPPOSITE: A fig species, *Ficus religiosa*, became known as the Bodhi tree after Buddha's experience at Bodh Gaya, and the trees continue to be revered by Buddhists and planted at temples.

thing and knew that he was close to achieving his goal of enlightenment. He would combine this understanding with the discipline of meditation. Sitting under the tree, he vowed to meditate, remaining perfectly still, until the wisdom he knew was coming filled his mind.

According to myth, the demon god Mara and an army of demons appeared before Siddhartha. Mara did not want Siddhartha to achieve enlightenment. He knew that enlightenment would erase desire from the world, and he didn't want this to happen.

Mara's demons attacked Siddhartha with arrows, but Siddhartha's peaceful heart caused the arrows to turn into flower blossoms. Next, Mara sent his three beautiful daughters to tempt Siddhartha, but Siddhartha did not move from his position beneath the fig tree. Frustrated, Mara challenged Siddhartha to prove that he deserved enlightenment. Mara's demons stood ready to attack should Siddhartha fail this final test. In silence, Siddhartha calmly reached his hand downward and touched the earth with his fingertips. The ground shook as Nature itself responded, signaling that Siddhartha was one with the world—a sign to Mara that Siddhartha was worthy of enlightenment. Having defeated Mara through peaceful resistance, Siddhartha continued to meditate.

Over the course of a night (or several weeks, depending on the story), Siddhartha became aware of his timeless

OPPOSITE The seated position taken in meditation and shown in most representations of Buddha is called lotus and is named after the flower, an Asian water lily; it is meant to promote calmness and quietness.

existence. The thoughts and feelings of thousands of past lives filled Siddhartha's mind and spirit. He was also flooded with an understanding of Samsāra and all the workings of the universe. In one translation of this experience, he states, "At this moment, all beings and I awakened together." This was the moment of enlightenment. He had entered the state of Nirvana, accepting that nothing exists beyond the present moment in an ever-changing universe, and with this acceptance, he felt neither suffering nor desire—only pure peace. By entering Nirvana, Siddhartha became the Buddha, and the tree under which he sat became known as the Bodhi tree—a symbol of enlightenment.

Overwhelmed by what he finally understood, Buddha was at first hesitant to tell anyone of his experience. He didn't think anyone would believe him. Myths tell of

OPPOSITE Brahma, with four faces and four arms, is depicted in Hindu art and architecture as holding symbols of creation: the sacred texts, prayer beads, and utensils for feeding sacrificial fire and obtaining water.

Brahma, the Hindu creator god, visiting Buddha. Brahma told Buddha that teaching people about his path to enlightenment would benefit the world. At Brahma's urging, Buddha set off to share his newfound wisdom. As he had expected, the first person he met did not believe him, but he persisted. He traveled to Sarnath, returning to the five ascetics with whom he had once lived. At first, they rejected him for giving up on asceticism. But when he explained how asceticism only clouds the mind and described his recent experiences, they embraced his ideas. He told them of his life as a pampered prince who felt spiritually empty. And he told them how asceticism had left him equally empty. Enlightenment, he explained, requires a balance between these two extremes—a lifestyle that would become known as the **Middle Way**. The five ascetics then became Buddha's first **monks**.

The Three Jewels

At the heart of Buddha's ideals are the Three Jewels. Buddha is represented by a yellow jewel. The Dharma (truth) is represented by a blue jewel. The Sangha (Buddhist community) is represented by a red jewel. Buddhists rely on Buddha as their teacher, the truth of his teachings as their spiritual guide, and the community of other Buddhists as their source of encouragement. This faith is called "taking refuge." An important Buddhist chant goes, "I take refuge in the Buddha, I take refuge in the Dharma, I take refuge in the Sangha."

The teachings of Buddha are called the *Dhamma*, a word that means "truth." Buddha's own journey to Nirvana had been long and arduous, and though he wished to spare his pupils from the same difficulties of discovery, he stressed to them that enlightenment could not be achieved easily or quickly. What filled his heart and mind could not be explained simply. It would take pupils time and commitment to understand the truth of his teachings. This truth is known as *Dharma*. He began by outlining the Four Noble Truths: (1) *Dukkha*, meaning that everything in life is craving and suffering; (2) *Samudaya*, meaning that suffering originates in the mind because we crave things that provide fleeting comfort; (3) *Norodha*, meaning that it is possible to stop the craving and suffering; and (4) *Magga*, meaning that there is a pathway to stopping the craving and suffering. The

Buddha then explained that this pathway is the Middle Way, also known as the Noble Eightfold Path.

Over the years, Buddha's followers grew in number, from a handful to hundreds and eventually thousands. Buddha's **monastic** order was called the Sangha. This community of Buddhist followers was open to everyone from kings to peasants, both men and women. The Sangha was a revolutionary idea, for in India, people from different castes did not mix, and women had few rights. In fact, many women found liberation in becoming Buddhist nuns. The success of the Sangha inspired Buddha to send his monks and nuns into distant lands to share his teachings. For 45 years, Buddha himself would crisscross an area of northern India about 250 miles (402 km) long and 150 miles (241 km) wide from the ancient cities of Kosambi in the west to Champapuri in the east.

When he was 80 years old, Buddha and some of his followers visited the home of a blacksmith named Chunda. When the men were offered a meal, Buddha did not allow his monks to eat. He alone ate what was offered and ordered the remaining food to be buried, for he sensed that the food was spoiled. Indeed, he became ill after eating. It is speculated that he developed **dysentery** from bacteria in the food. Chunda apologized for his grievous mistake, but the Buddha did not blame him. Instead, he praised Chunda. According to one translation of Buddha's words, he said, "It is to your merit, Chunda, that I am going to final Nirvana after taking this last meal from you. Two offerings of food are more meritorious than any other. The first is the one after eating which I attain supreme enlightenment, and the other after which I gain the Nirvana without remainder." Buddha knew

The Noble Eightfold Path

In Buddhist teaching, the parts of the Eightfold Path are not steps to be followed in order. Rather, they should be viewed as eight strands of a rope that work together. *Right speech* is to be truthful and kind with words. *Right action* is to be honorable and peaceful. *Right livelihood* is to never harm others—even animals. *Right effort* is to avoid negative thoughts. *Right mindfulness* is being aware of our thoughts and feelings. *Right concentration* is meditating to achieve an understanding of the self. *Right thought* is thinking only about kindness and nonviolence. *Right understanding* is an understanding of the Four Noble Truths. A Buddhist follows, practices, and develops a way of life that embraces all elements of the Eightfold Path.

OPPOSITE The Buddhist term *parinirvana* indicates the final deathless state, the release from Samsāra, that occurs when the body of a person who has achieved Nirvana in his or her lifetime dies.

that upon his death, he would finally be released from Samsāra. After traveling a short distance toward the town of Kushinagar the next day, Buddha bathed in the Kukuta River and then lay down in a grove of sal trees. His disciples gathered around, crying. Buddha knew he was dying. He told his disciples they should not let his teachings die with him, nor should they revere him as a god. He told them, "For that which I have proclaimed and made known as the Dhamma and the Discipline, that shall be your Master when I am gone."

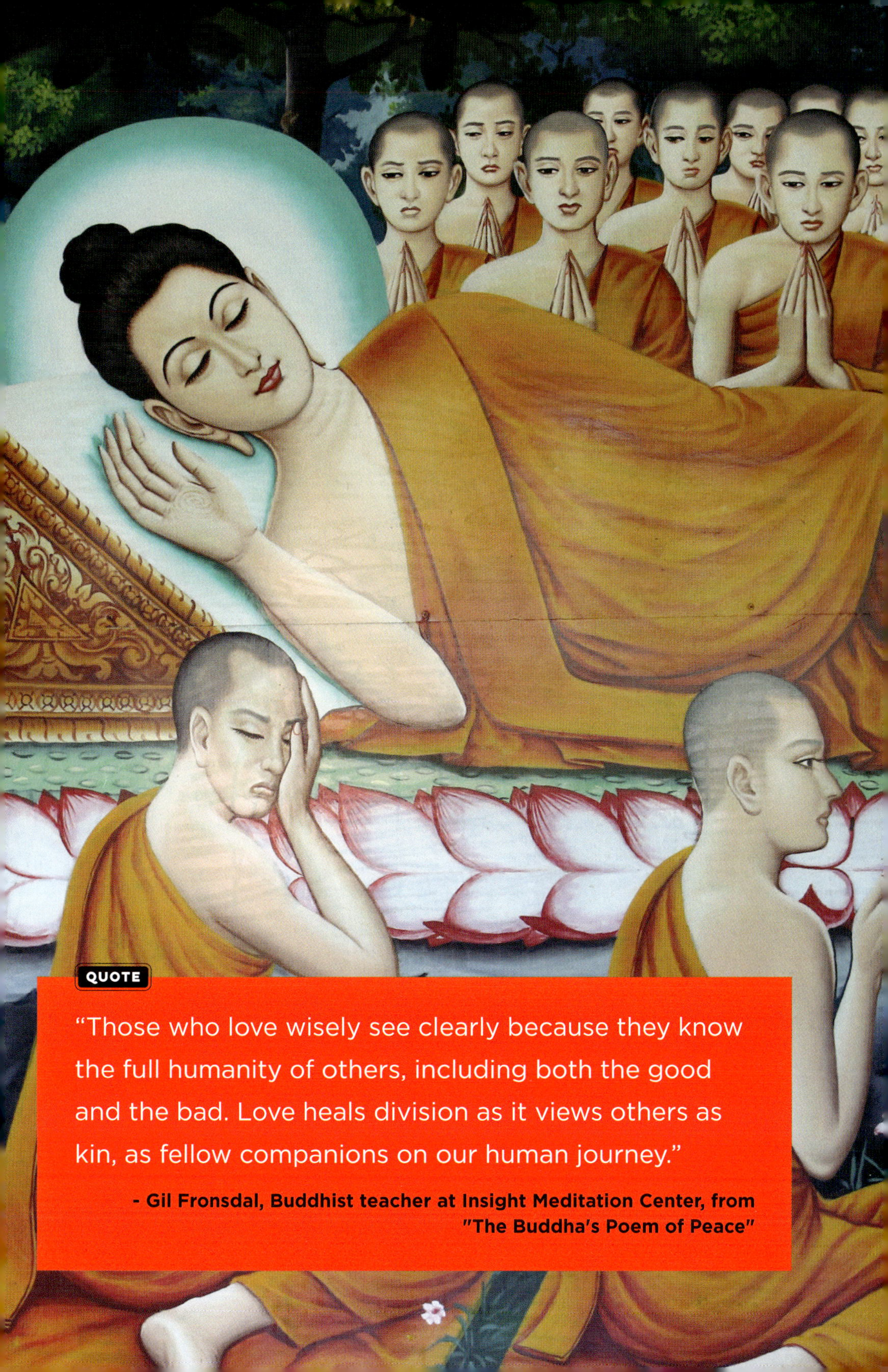

QUOTE

"Those who love wisely see clearly because they know the full humanity of others, including both the good and the bad. Love heals division as it views others as kin, as fellow companions on our human journey."

- Gil Fronsdal, Buddhist teacher at Insight Meditation Center, from "The Buddha's Poem of Peace"

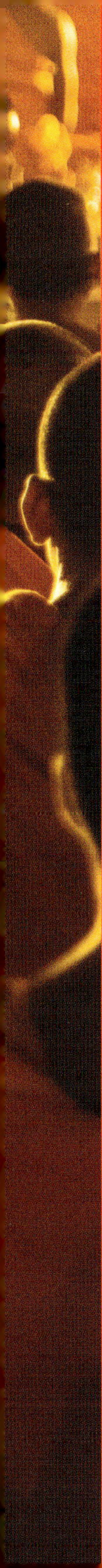

Path to Peace

The Dhamma comprises roughly 84,000 Buddhist teachings. These sacred scriptures, collected in three parts, are together called the *Dhammapada*. The parts are the *Sutta* (Buddha's lessons), the *Vinaya* (Buddha's rules for monks and nuns), and the *Abhidhamma* (explanations of Buddha's lessons). They were first delivered orally and passed down through the generations. The earliest written versions of the scriptures

OPPOSITE: Buddhist monks and nuns shave their heads and put on the robes when they start their training, and they also promise to abandon their attachments to social conventions—including money.

TAKEAWAY

In Pali, the word *ti* means "three," and *pitaka* means "basket." Pali is the language of Theravada, the younger of the two branches of Buddhism.

appeared about 100 B.C., when Buddhist monks and nuns began writing them on palm leaves. These leaves were carried in baskets. For this reason, the scriptures were named the *Tipitaka*. In Pali, the word *ti* means "three," and *pitaka* means "basket." Pali is the language of Theravada, the younger of the two branches of Buddhism. The word *Pali* itself means "school of the elder monks." Buddha's lessons were also translated into Sanskrit, which is the traditional language of Mahayana, the older branch of Buddhism. Today, the entire *Tipitaka* is collected in 45 to 56 volumes, depending on the translation.

Similar to the way Christianity eventually split into Catholic and Protestant branches, the division of Buddhism into two branches was based on a combination of politics, geography, and differing cultural interpretations of the sacred scriptures. Distinctions between the two major branches of Buddhism began to take shape around 100 B.C. All Buddhists agree on the general principles of the Four Noble Truths and the Noble Eightfold Path, but some of the major differences between Mahayana and Theravada Buddhism focus on rituals and behaviors. For example, many Mahayana Buddhists are strict vegetarians, refusing to harm animals in any way, but Theravada Buddhists do not follow this rule—mostly because their local food supply has traditionally made it difficult to do so. Also, Mahayana Buddhist rituals

The Mustard Seeds

A woman named Kisa Gotami's only child died. Devastated, she went to Buddha to ask if he could restore her son's life. He told her to go to her village and gather mustard seeds from every family who had never been touched by death. With those seeds, Buddha promised he could bring Kisa's son back to life. All the villagers wanted to give Kisa mustard seeds, but they all told her that their families had been touched by death. Finally, Kisa realized what Buddha wanted her to know: death touches everyone. She grieved for her child and buried him in the forest.

OPPOSITE Self-exiled from Tibet since 1959, the 14th Dalai Lama lives in McLeod Ganj, near Dharamshala, India, where he was in the habit of giving biannual teachings.

for worship tend to be quite elaborate, but Theravada worship is modest and simple. And while a person's connection to nature is strongly emphasized in Mahayana Buddhism, it is absent from the Theravada tradition. In his many talks on Buddhism, His Holiness the 14th **Dalai Lama** has stressed the point that Buddha created no strict doctrine, no hard and fast rules for non-monastic followers. In fact, Buddha argued against the following of any religious authority or tradition for its own sake. Rather, Buddha wanted his followers to interpret and practice his teachings in relation to their own cultural heritage, using logical reasoning to follow the Eightfold Path in ways that fit their individual lives.

As a mendicant, Buddha demonstrated the value of traveling to both seek and share spiritual fulfillment. For this reason, many Buddhists recognize **pilgrimage** as

an important component of their practice. Four major Buddhist pilgrimage sites exist in India. According to the *Tipitaka,* these sites were named by Buddha himself as places where his followers would find encouragement. Lumbini, the birthplace of the infant Siddhartha, is near the modern city of Bhairahawa, just across the Indian border in Nepal. The site is considered a cultural treasure and has been listed by the United Nations Educational, Scientific and Cultural Organization (UNESCO) as a World Heritage Site, meaning it will be preserved "for the benefit of humanity." The site is home to a number of structures, including the Shakya Tank, the pool where Siddhartha's mother is believed to have bathed before Siddhartha's birth. Also at the site are the Maya Devi Temple and an Ashoka pillar. Around 260 B.C., Ashoka, India's greatest king, erected a temple and the accompanying 54-foot (16.5 m) stone pillar topped with lions facing the four directions. The lions symbolize Buddha's first teaching—the Four Noble Truths.

Another pilgrimage site—considered the most important—is Bodh Gaya. Here, a huge fig tree grows in the Mahabodhi Temple complex in the spot where it is believed that Buddha attained enlightenment. The tree is believed to be a descendant of the fig tree under which Buddha sat. In 2002, the Mahabodhi Temple became a UNESCO World Heritage Site. In Sarnath, the Dhamek Stupa stands in the spot believed to be the place where Buddha gave his first teaching of the Four Noble Truths to the five ascetics. This is another pilgrimage site of great importance to Buddhists because it was here that the Sangha was founded. An earlier structure had been built by King Ashoka around 249 B.C., but it

OPPOSITE The structure of the Mahabodhi Temple is pyramidal with an ornamental stupa at the top; stupas were traditionally hemispherical or mound-shaped places for storing relics of the Buddha.

fell into disrepair and was rebuilt in the A.D. 500s. Today, the Sarnath Museum, established in 1910, is home to nearly 7,000 Indian sculptures and artifacts dating from the 3rd to the 12th centuries—many related to Buddha. The fourth major pilgrimage site is Kushinagar, the place where Buddha died and was **cremated**. The first part of the Parinirvana Stupa was built shortly after Buddha's death but was rebuilt and greatly expanded to include a temple hundreds of years later. A modern temple was built on the site in 1956.

Buddhism is viewed by many people as a religion. Others think of it as a philosophy or simply a way of life. Buddha's dying words to his followers were that he not be revered as a god but that his example of compassion be followed. A number of contemporary social and political leaders have modeled Buddha's peaceful humility and

The Boys and the Snake

While traveling from the ancient city of Shravasti to the Jetavana monastery, Buddha encountered a group of boys hitting a snake with a stick. The boys appeared to be enjoying this activity, which saddened Buddha. He approached them and said, “All tremble at the rod. All fear death. Comparing others with oneself, one should neither strike nor cause others to strike.” Buddha taught the boys about compassion by asking them to consider how they would feel about being the victims of violence.

Defend with Compassion

Buddha taught that a person should ignore taunting and insults, but if someone is physically attacked, self-defense is allowed—as long as that defense is performed with compassion. As he told his monks, "Even if bandits were to carve you up savagely, limb by limb, with a two-handled saw, he among you who let his heart get angered even at that would not be doing my bidding. Say, 'Our minds will be unaffected, and we will say no evil words. We will remain sympathetic, with a mind of goodwill, and with no inner hate.'"

respect for all living beings. Among them are Mahatma Gandhi, who, in the early 20th century, led the nation of India to freedom from British colonialism, mainly by means of peaceful resistance. Inspired by Gandhi's success in the use of nonviolence to achieve social change, South African president **Nelson Mandela** committed himself to finding peaceful solutions to his nation's racial conflicts. As Buddha spoke in the *Dhammapada*, "Hatred never ends with hatred. By love alone does it end. This is an ancient truth." Just as Buddha had intended, his message that all living beings are connected and deserving of equal respect is a value that is shared by hundreds of millions of people—both Buddhists and non-Buddhists alike—in nearly every part of the world today.

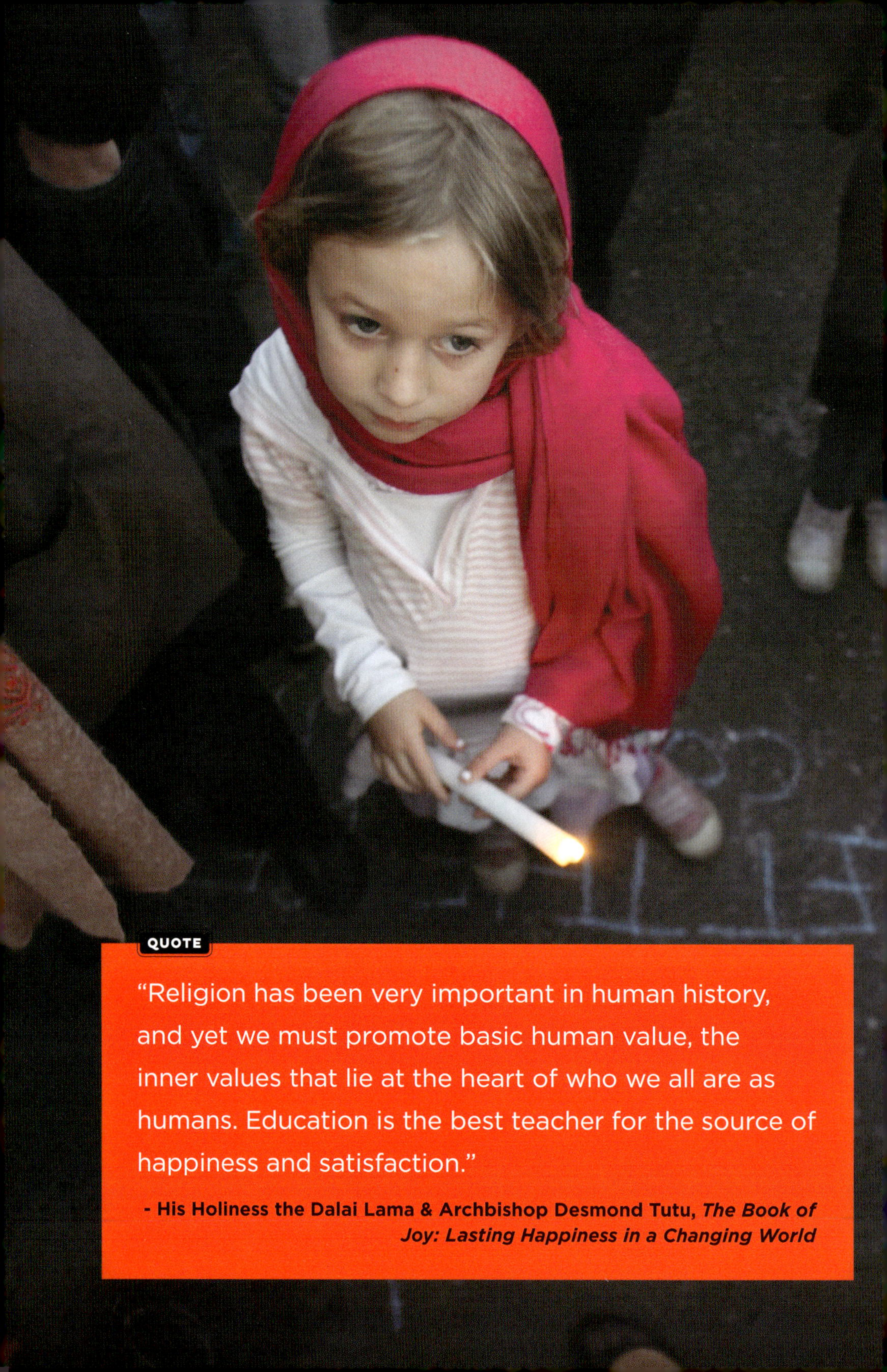

QUOTE

"Religion has been very important in human history, and yet we must promote basic human value, the inner values that lie at the heart of who we all are as humans. Education is the best teacher for the source of happiness and satisfaction."

- His Holiness the Dalai Lama & Archbishop Desmond Tutu, *The Book of Joy: Lasting Happiness in a Changing World*

Timeline

563 B.C. Siddhartha Gautama is born, legendarily emerging from his mother's side.

547 B.C. Siddhartha marries his cousin Yasodhara.

534 B.C. Siddhartha's son is born; Siddhartha leaves his wife and child to seek answers to life's questions.

533 B.C. Siddhartha becomes the pupil of the gurus Ālāra Kālāma and Uddaka Rāmaputta, with whom he masters the art of meditation.

532 B.C. Dissatisfied with the impermanence of meditation, Siddhartha practices asceticism for the next six years.

526 B.C. Siddhartha meditates under the Bodhi tree and attains enlightenment, becoming the Buddha.

526 B.C. Siddhartha receives rice milk from Sujata, which is his first step toward returning to health.

526 B.C. Buddha travels to Sarnath, where he delivers his first teaching to his former companions, the five ascetics; they become his first disciples.

525 B.C. The first Buddhist monastery, the Bamboo Grove Monastery, is established near Venuvana in what is today the Indian state of Bihar.

523 B.C. For seven days, Buddha visits his father, Suddhodana, on his deathbed and helps him achieve peace before his death.

514 B.C. Buddha creates the *Vinaya*, sharing these rules with his monks and nuns.

483 B.C. While teaching in the town of Beluva, Buddha falls ill, perhaps with pneumonia; he recovers but remains feeble.

483 B.C. At age 80, Buddha dies near the town of Kushinagar, most likely from food poisoning.

Selected Bibliography

Blomfield, Vishvapani. *Gautama Buddha: The Life and Teachings of the Awakened One.* New York: Quercus, 2011.

Bodhi, Bhikkuh, ed. *In Buddha's Words: An Anthology of Discourses from the Pāli Canon.* Somerville, Mass.: Wisdom Publications, 2005.

Karlsson, Klemens. "The Formation of Early Buddhist Visual Culture. *Material Religion* 2, no. 1 (March 2006): 68–95, DOI: 10.2752/174322006778053906.

Landaw, Jonathan, and Janet Brooke. *Prince Siddhartha: The Story of Buddha.* Somerville, Mass.: Wisdom Publications, 2011.

Mandel Khan, Gabriel. *Buddha: The Enlightened One.* San Diego: Thunder Bay Press, 2005.

Mehwood, Rasib, and Shaheen Khan. "Siddhartha: A Modern Man of Ancient India." *A Research Journal of South Asian Studies* 33, no.1 (January-June 2018): 315–324.

"The Path of Awakening." *The Pluralism Project.* Harvard University. http://pluralism.org/religions/buddhism/introduction-to-buddhism/the-path-of-awakening/.

Sen, Amartya. "The Contemporary Relevance of Buddha." *Ethics & International Affairs* 28, no. 1 (January 2014): 15–27, DOI: 10.1017/S0892679414000033.

Endnotes

ascetic a person who gives up material possessions and severely limits food, shelter, and other necessities, typically for religious or spiritual reasons

caste a social class into which one is born; the Hindu caste system was based on the purest people (priests) being at the top

celestial of or relating to natural objects in space visible to the naked eye or through astronomical equipment

cremated burned completely to ashes

cultural relativism the concept that people's beliefs, values, and behaviors should be understood on the basis of their own history and culture and not judged against other cultures

Dalai Lama the spiritual leader of Tibetan Buddhism and, until the establishment of Chinese rule over Tibet, the political leader of Tibet

dysentery an infection of the intestines resulting in severe diarrhea and abdominal pain; caused by bacteria, viruses, or parasites

enlightenment in Buddhism, a state of supreme knowledge of truth and compassion that leads to an end of suffering; also known as Nirvana

Hinduism both a cultural way of life and the world's third-largest religion, with four denominations that revere various gods and goddesses; the foremost Hindu sacred texts are the *Vedas*, or "Books of Knowledge"

mendicant a person who travels from city to city to preach religion or teach spirituality while remaining unemployed and living in poverty

Middle Way in Buddhism, a lifestyle that balances the extremes of self-indulgence and self-denial

monastic relating to monks, nuns, or others living under prescribed religious discipline

monks members of a religious community of men typically living under established vows based on humility; female monks are called nuns

myths popular, traditional beliefs or stories that explain how something came to be or are associated with a person or object

Nelson Mandela (1918–2013)—South African lawyer and politician who led an antiapartheid campaign; after spending 27 years in jail, he served as president of South Africa from 1994 to 1999

pilgrimage a journey, especially a long one, for purposes of visiting places of cultural or religious importance

Samsāra the endless cycle of death and rebirth in Hindu tradition; commonly known as reincarnation

yoga from the Sanskrit *yug*, meaning "to join together"; a system of breathing techniques, meditation, and body postures meant to enable the joining of the physical and spiritual bodies

Websites

Dhammatalks
https://www.dhammatalks.org

Learn more about the teachings of Buddha through text and audio translations of the *Dhammapada*.

Siddhartha Buddha
https://www.ancient.eu/Siddhartha_Gautama/

Discover the myths, legends, and legacy of Buddha through text and video.

Note: Every effort has been made to ensure that any websites listed above were active at the time of publication. However, because of the nature of the Internet, it is impossible to guarantee that these sites will remain active indefinitely or that their contents will not be altered.

Index